#24017

Lexile 820

Careers without College

Occupational Therapy Aide

by Kathryn A. Quinlan

Consultant:

Kathleen Matuska, M.P.H., O.T.R.
Assistant Professor, Occupational Therapy Department
College of St. Catherine
St. Paul, Minnesota

CAPSTONE
HIGH/LOW BOOKS
an imprint of Capstone Press
Mankato, Minnesota

Capstone High/Low Books are published by Capstone Press
818 North Willow Street • Mankato, Minnesota 56001
http://www.capstone-press.com

Library of Congress Cataloging-in-Publication Data
Quinlan, Kathryn A.
  Occupational therapy aide/by Kathryn A. Quinlan.
    p. cm.—(Careers without college)
  Includes bibliographical references and index.
  Summary: Describes the job responsibilities and work environment of occupational
therapy aides as well as the necessary training, job outlook, salary, and career potential.
  ISBN 0-7368-0037-9
  1. Occupational therapy assistants—Vocational guidance—Juvenile literature.
[1. Allied health personnel—Vocational guidance. 2. Vocational guidance.] I. Title.
II. Series: Careers without college (Mankato, Minn.)
RM735.4.Q56 1999
615.8'515'023—dc21   98-7184
                                                                                   CIP
                                                                                    AC

Editorial Credits
Kimberly J. Graber and Angela Kaelberer, editors; James Franklin, cover designer
    and illustrator; Sheri Gosewisch, photo researcher
Photo Credits
David F. Clobes, 4, 6, 9, 12, 14, 19, 20, 22, 24, 28, 30, 32, 44, 47
Leslie O'Shaughnessy, 11, 38
Meinhardt Photography/Gretchen Meinhardt, 34
New England Stock Photo/Frank Siteman, 36
Unicorn Stock Photos/Dennis McDonald, 27
Uniphoto/Charles Gupton, cover
Visuals Unlimited/Jeff Greenberg, 16, 43

Table of Contents

Fast Facts 5

Chapter 1 Job Responsibilities 7

Chapter 2 What the Job Is Like 17

Chapter 3 Training. 25

Chapter 4 Salary and Job Outlook 29

Chapter 5 Where the Job Can Lead 35

Words to Know 40

To Learn More 42

Useful Addresses 45

Internet Sites 46

Index 48

Fast Facts

Career Title_____ Occupational therapy aide

Minimum Educational_____ U.S.: high school diploma
Requirement   Canada: some high school *

Certification Requirement_____ U.S.: none
                                Canada: none *

Salary Range_____ U.S.: $13,520 to $15,600
(U.S. Bureau of Labor Statistics and   Canada: $15,400 to $46,400 *
Human Resources Development Canada,   (Canadian dollars)
late 1990s figures)

Job Outlook_____ U.S.: faster than average growth
(U.S. Bureau of Labor Statistics and   Canada: good *
Human Resources Development
Canada, late 1990s projections)

DOT Cluster_____ Service occupations
(Dictionary of Occupational Titles)

DOT Number_____ 355.377-010

GOE Number_____ 10.03.02
(Guide for Occupational Exploration)

NOC_____ 6631
(National Occupational Classification—Canada)

*Information applies to all health aides and assistants

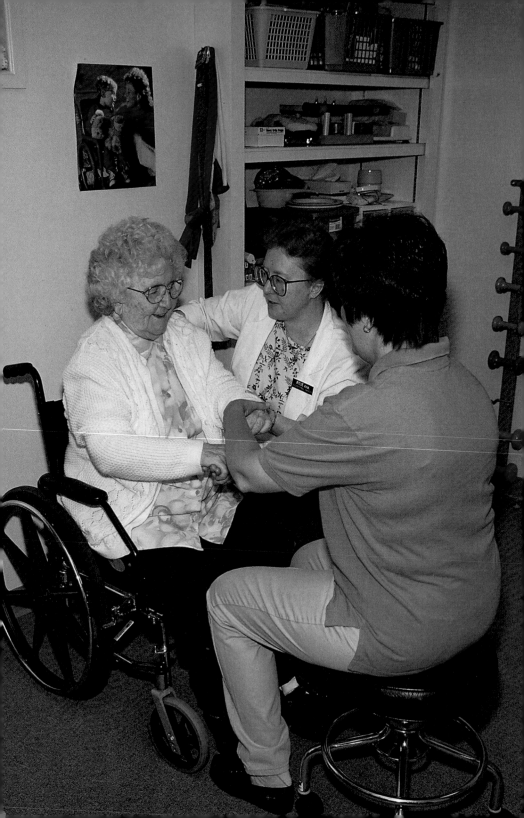

Chapter 1

Job Responsibilities

Occupational therapy aides help occupational therapy practitioners work with patients who have disabilities. Occupational therapy practitioners and occupational therapy aides help patients become independent or prepare for jobs. Occupational therapy providers help patients overcome their disabilities. Patients learn to perform everyday tasks in occupational therapy.

Occupational therapy aides help occupational therapy practitioners work with patients who have disabilities.

Patients may have disabilities because they have been hurt or ill. They may have been born with limited use of their bodies or minds. Occupational therapy patients may have developed disabilities as they grew older.

Occupational Therapy Practitioners

Occupational therapy is a type of treatment for rehabilitating patients. The aim of occupational therapy is to help patients regain their health and abilities. Some patients cannot completely regain their abilities. Occupational therapy practitioners help these patients learn to live with their challenges. For example, occupational therapy practitioners may help people who are in wheelchairs learn to dress themselves.

Occupational therapy practitioners use activities to help patients recover or improve their skills. Practitioners plan activities that match each patient's needs. For example, one patient may have unsteadiness in the hands and arms. The

Occupational therapy is a type of treatment for rehabilitating patients.

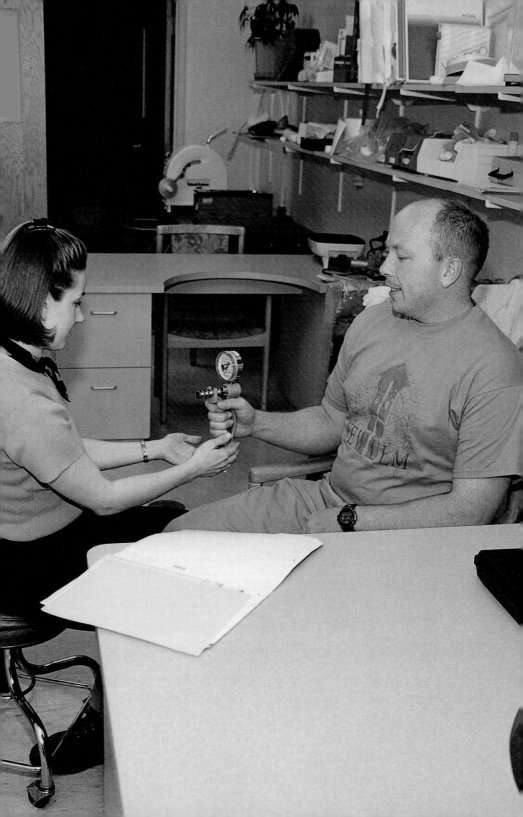

practitioner might recommend that this patient use silverware with special handles. The special handles would help the patient eat independently. Another patient may need to learn to prepare food. The practitioner might plan for this patient to buy ingredients and bake cookies.

Occupational therapy practitioners teach people to use tools that help them adapt to changes. For example, a practitioner may teach a patient how to bathe using a bath chair.

Occupational therapy practitioners help patients gain job skills. Practitioners teach patients to use tools that help them work. A person who cannot hear may use a telephone that prints words. Public travel can be hard for people who use wheelchairs or who have learning disabilities. Occupational therapy practitioners teach patients how to use buses or trains to go to work.

On the Job
Occupational therapy aides work under the very close supervision of occupational therapy

Occupational therapy practitioners use activities to help patients recover or improve their skills.

practitioners. Aides perform many tasks so practitioners can spend most of their time with patients. Aides assemble materials used for therapy. They gather supplies for activities and clean up after activities. Many aides also keep lists of all supplies. They check these lists to decide when to order new supplies.

Occupational therapy aides keep patients' files in order. Occupational therapy practitioners keep files on each patient. They write down patients' needs and special problems in these files. They note the methods used to help patients. Practitioners check these files to see if patients are improving.

Occupational therapy aides perform general office tasks. They may transport patients to and from the therapy room. Many aides answer telephones and schedule appointments. Aides may fill out forms for health insurance companies. People pay money to insurance

Occupational therapy aides keep patients' files in order.

companies each month. Insurance companies pay most of the bills if people need health care.

Some aides work with patients. But only occupational therapy practitioners decide what patients need. Practitioners plan activities that will help patients. Aides follow practitioners' instructions. Aides work under occupational therapy practitioners' supervision.

Aides may work closely with patients during planned activities. Aides may help patients learn or relearn cooking skills by helping patients measure ingredients. Patients may need help from aides to hold silverware as they learn to feed themselves.

Occupational therapy aides may help patients learn or relearn cooking skills.

Chapter 2

What the Job Is Like

Many occupational therapy aides work in places where older people receive care. These include nursing homes or residential care centers. People who live in these centers have personal care and medical care available when they need it.

Occupational therapy aides have jobs in many other types of places. Hospitals need

Many occupational therapy aides work in places where older people receive care.

aides. Some aides work in schools. Other aides work in clinics and occupational therapy practitioners' offices. Outpatient rehabilitation centers also hire occupational therapy aides. Outpatients do not stay overnight.

Work Environment

Occupational therapy aides may choose from many work schedules. Some occupational therapy aides have full-time jobs. These aides work 40 hours each week. Other aides work part-time. Most aides work during the day. Some aides work at night or on weekends.

Occupational therapy aides who work with patients may work with children, adults, or older people. Some aides help children learn new skills. Some aides help older patients with activities that keep their minds and bodies active. Aides who work in hospitals work with people of all ages. These aides help people

Some occupational therapy aides work in schools.

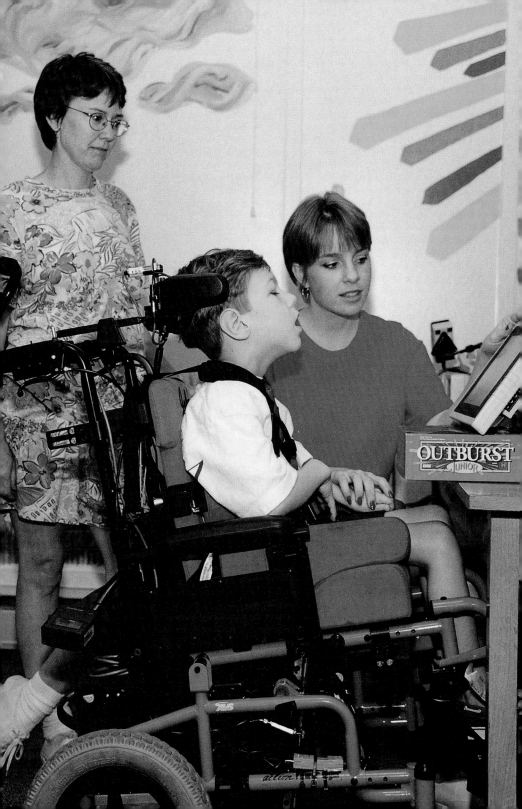

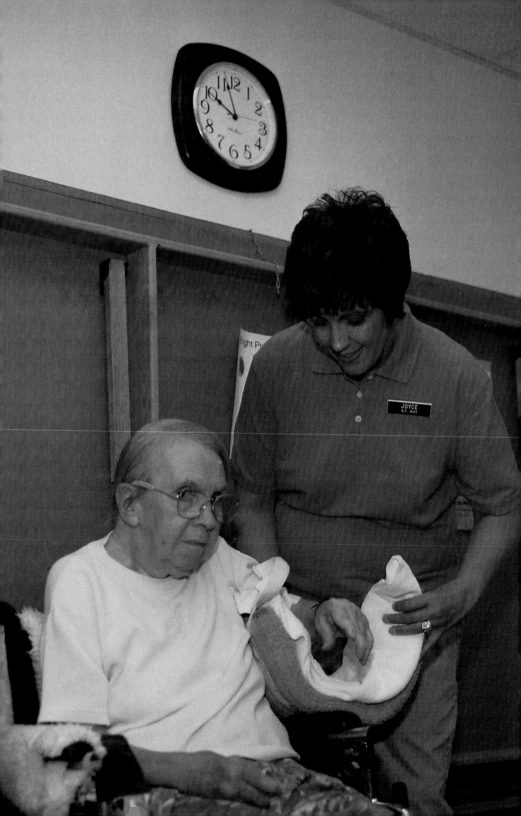

recover from illnesses or wounds. Aides help people adapt to new challenges.

Occupational therapy aides do not have easy jobs. Their days can be tiring. They may have to lift heavy files or spend many hours working on computers. Patients may need aides' help to dress and brush their teeth. Aides often must lift patients or help them move.

Most occupational therapy aides enjoy their work because they know they help people. Aides help patients gain the strength and skills they need to reach their goals.

Personal Qualities

Occupational therapy aides should be helpful and caring. Patients may find it hard to perform simple tasks. They may perform some tasks very slowly. Patients often feel helpless and upset. Aides must be able to help and encourage these patients.

Occupational therapy aides help people adapt to new challenges.

Patients sometimes need to talk about their feelings. Occupational therapy aides must be good listeners. They should be cheerful and friendly.

Most aides work with occupational therapy practitioners, doctors, nurses, and nurse assistants. This means aides must be able to work well in teams. They must be polite to co-workers and patients. They must be able to follow directions from others.

Occupational therapy aides should be organized. They must be good at keeping supplies and files in order. Organized supplies and files are easier for other people to find.

Occupational therapy aides should be organized.

Chapter 3

Training

People do not need formal training or college degrees to become occupational therapy aides. Aides in the United States must have high school diplomas. Aides in Canada should have some high school education. Employers require training on the job. They also may require additional education.

Training on the Job
Occupational therapy aides learn their jobs from occupational therapy practitioners. They learn how to help patients perform activities that practitioners plan. Aides may help record patients'

Occupational therapy aides learn their jobs from occupational therapy practitioners.

progress. They learn how to organize records and supplies.

Aides may learn more difficult tasks as their careers advance. They may learn more about working with patients. Aides do not have licenses to treat clients. This means practitioners must always oversee aides as they work with patients. Most states have laws regulating the work aides are allowed to do.

What Students Can Do Now

Students can prepare to be occupational therapy aides while they are in high school. Basic computer and office skills are important for occupational therapy aides. Students can take keyboarding and computer classes to gain these skills. Occupational therapy aides also must be strong and fit. Other important classes include sciences, health, art, social sciences, and physical education.

Students also can learn skills by volunteering at hospitals or nursing homes. Volunteers offer to do a job without pay. Volunteers may be able to watch

Basic computer and office skills are important for occupational therapy aides.

occupational therapy aides work. They can find out if they enjoy helping people.

Volunteers also can meet people who hire occupational therapy aides. These people often will help volunteers find jobs.

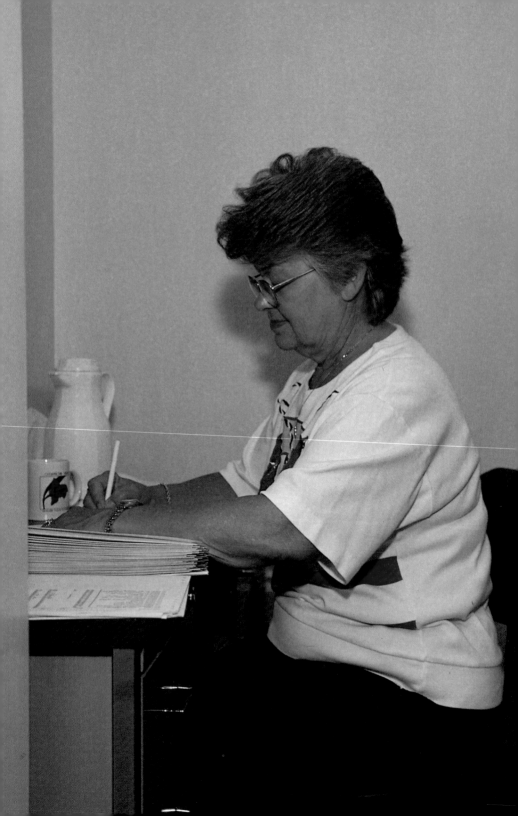

Chapter 4

Salary and Job Outlook

Beginning full-time occupational therapy aides in the United States earn from $13,520 to $15,600 per year (all figures late 1990s). Full-time health aides and assistants in Canada earn from $15,400 to $46,400 per year. Assistants earn higher wages because of their education. Aides usually are paid by the hour. They can earn more money as they gain experience.

Occupational therapy aides can earn more money as they gain experience.

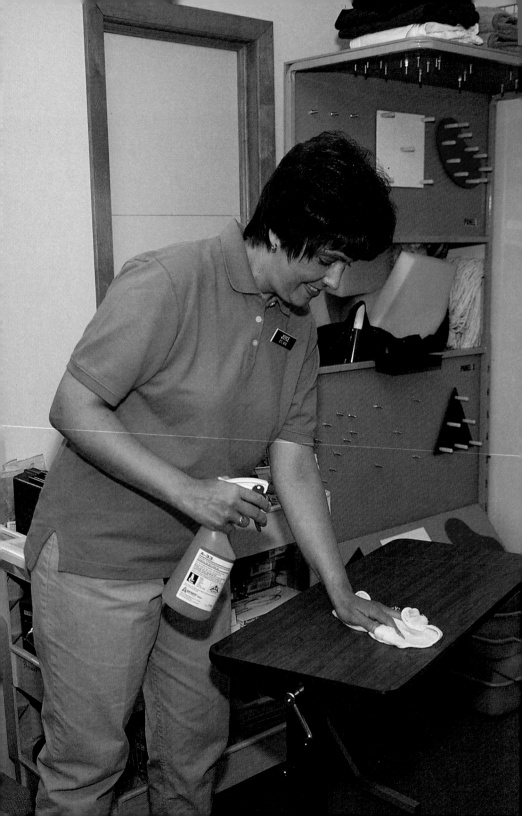

Job Outlook

Occupational therapy is a growing field. The number of jobs for occupational therapy aides also is growing. But the job field is still small.

Hospitals and nursing homes must meet the growing need for occupational therapy. They are hiring more occupational therapy aides to meet this need. Aides perform tasks that save time for occupational therapy practitioners. This means practitioners can treat more patients.

Why the Field Is Growing

Today, people live longer than in the past. People sometimes become hurt or disabled as they age. This means that more people need occupational therapy.

The field also is growing because of advances in medicine. Doctors save more people from serious wounds or illnesses than in the past. But the people who are affected

Occupational therapy aides perform tasks that save time for occupational therapy practitioners.

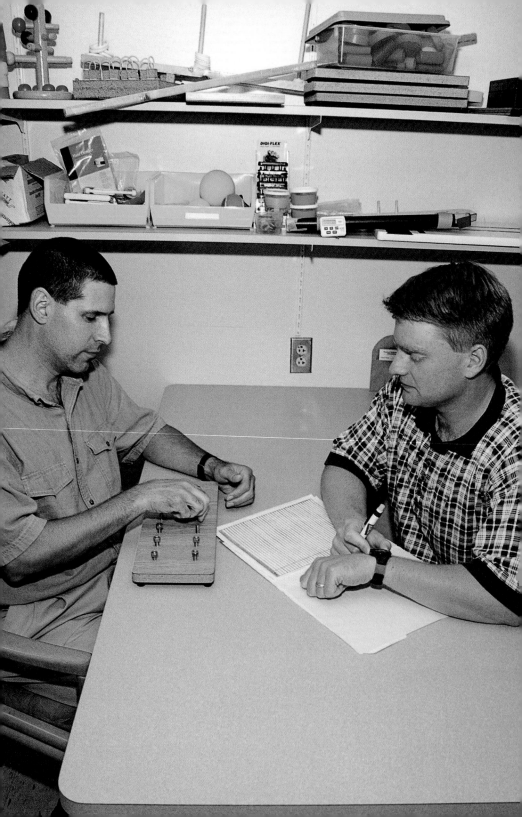

by wounds or illnesses often need to be rehabilitated. Occupational therapy helps them adapt to new challenges.

In the United States, people with disabilities now are able to get better jobs than in the past. The U.S. government passed the Americans with Disabilities Act in 1990. This law protects the rights of people with disabilities. It says employers cannot use disability as a reason to deny anyone a job. People affected by this act are joining the work force. Occupational therapy helps people with disabilities prepare for jobs.

Occupational therapy helps people with disabilities prepare for jobs.

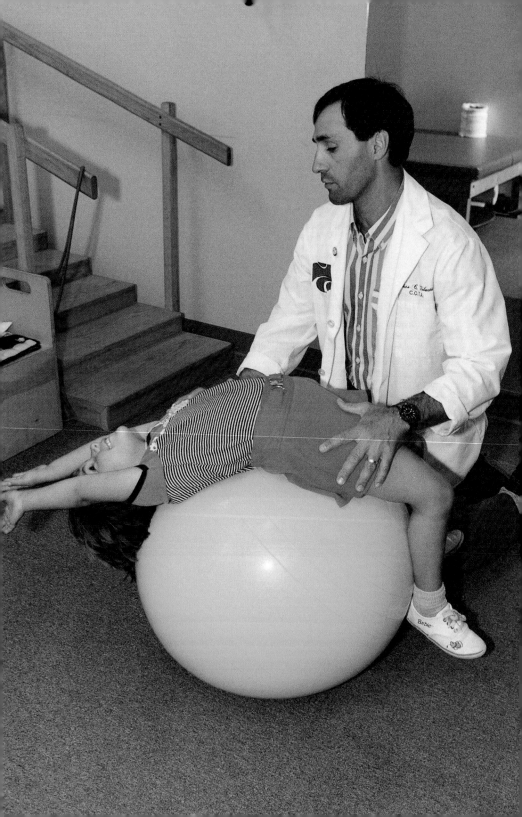

Chapter 5

Where the Job Can Lead

Occupational therapy aides can advance in several ways. Those who have worked for several years may work with patients more often. Aides may be able to earn more money by changing locations. Jobs in larger cities may pay more.

Occupational Therapy Assistants
With training and education, some aides may advance to become occupational therapy

With training and education, some aides may advance to become occupational therapy assistants.

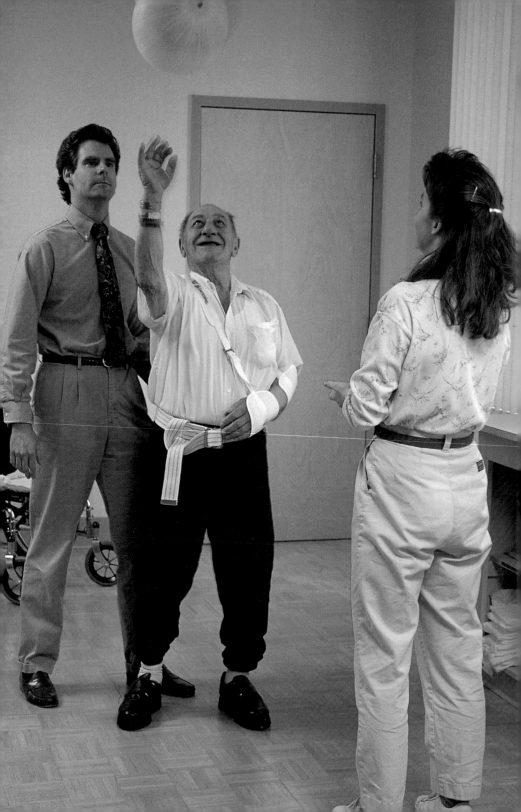

assistants. Assistants work closely with occupational therapists. They work with patients more than aides do. Occupational therapy assistants often assist in the supervision of occupational therapy aides. They earn more money than aides earn because they have more training and responsibilities.

An occupational therapy assistant must have a degree from a community college. Occupational therapy assistants attend college for about two years. Students in occupational therapy programs study basic health care. They also study more specific areas such as anatomy and mental health. Anatomy classes teach students about the human body. Mental health classes teach students about the human mind. Occupational therapy assistants also study health care for children and older people.

Occupational therapy assistants must complete at least three months of fieldwork before they can get jobs. These work experiences

Occupational therapy assistants often assist in the supervision of occupational therapy aides.

allow students to learn the job by working with experts in the field. Assistants also must be certified. This means they have officially recognized skills and abilities. Occupational therapy assistants must pass a written test to become certified.

Occupational Therapists

Some occupational therapy aides decide to become occupational therapists. An occupational therapist must earn a four-year university degree. Some have higher degrees. Occupational therapists also must pass a written test to be certified.

Occupational therapists oversee assistants and aides. They plan activities for patients. They watch patients' progress. Some occupational therapists work in their own offices. Some work in patients' homes. Some work in schools, hospitals, nursing homes, and clinics. Aides who enjoy working in the occupational therapy field may want to advance into this career.

Some occupational therapists work in their own offices.

Words to Know

certified (SUR-ti-fide)—officially recognized for skills and abilities

degree (di-GREE)—a title a person receives for completing a course of study at a college or university

disability (diss-uh-BIL-uh-tee)—something that restricts people in what they can do, usually because of an illness, injury, or condition present at birth

fieldwork (FEELD-wurk)—a job that allows a student to learn from an expert in the field

health insurance (HELTH in-SHUR-uhnss)—protection from the costs of health care

license (LYE-suhnss)—a document that provides official permission to do something

rehabilitate (ree-huh-BIL-uh-tayt)—to return to health or activity

therapy (THER-uh-pee)—a treatment for an illness, an injury, or a disability

volunteer (vol-uhn-TIHR)—to offer to do a job without pay

To Learn More

Abbott, Marguerite, Marie-Louise Franciscus, Zona R. Weeks. *Opportunities in Occupational Therapy Careers.* VGM Opportunities. Lincolnwood, Ill.: VGM Career Horizons, 1995.

Snook, I. Donald, Jr. *Opportunities in Health and Medical Careers.* VGM Opportunities. Lincolnwood, Ill.: VGM Career Horizons, 1998.

Wilkinson, Beth. *Careers inside the World of Health Care.* New York: Rosen Publishing Group, 1995.

Useful Addresses

American Occupational Therapy Association
4720 Montgomery Lane
Bethesda, MD 20814-3425

**Canadian Association
    of Occupational Therapists**
1125 Colonel By Drive
Suite 3400
Ottawa, Ontario K1S 5R1
Canada

**National Board for Certification in
    Occupational Therapy**
800 S. Frederick Avenue
Suite 200
Gaithersburg, MD 20877-4150

Internet Sites

American Occupational Therapy Association
http://www.aota.org

Canada Job Futures—
Elemental Medical and Hospital Assistants
http://www.hrdc-drhc.gc.ca/JobFutures/english/
volume1/663/663.htm

Canadian Association of
Occupational Therapists
http://www.caot.ca/welcome.html

Occupational Outlook Handbook—
Occupational Therapy Assistants and Aides
http://stats.bls.gov/oco/ocos166.htm

Index

activities, 8, 13, 15, 18, 25, 39

clinics, 18, 39
college, 37
computers, 21

disability, 7, 8, 10, 33

education, 25, 26, 29, 35
experience, 29, 37

fieldwork, 37
files, 13, 21, 23

hospitals, 17, 18, 26, 31, 39

insurance companies, 13, 15

licenses, 26

nursing homes, 17, 26, 31, 39

occupational therapist, 37, 39
occupational therapy assistant, 35, 37, 39

responsibilities, 37

skills, 8, 10, 15, 18, 21, 26, 39
supplies, 13, 23, 26

training, 25, 35, 37
treatment, 8

volunteers, 26, 27